Screaming Off Key

Gracie Borjas

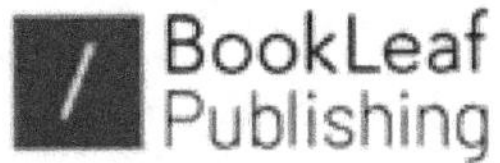

Presentation by *BookLeaf Publishing*

Web: www.bookleafpub.com

E-mail: info@bookleafpub.com

ISBN: 9789357211345

First edition 2022

DEDICATION

My babies, who always have a laugh to share.
You are egg-cellent.

Culture

I try to carry my culture on my skin.
Let the history of my ancestors be written on my
flesh.
Their sun kissed bronze skin from working in
the fields defies my paleness.
The laboring hands that raised my father look
nothing like the uncalloused palms of my own.
I do not "look" Latina.
My Spanish is only mediocre, my English
without accent.
Don't tell me I "talk white".
Show me the wisdom of my people.
Show me the love, community, curiosity and
spirit of learning that runs through our veins
Let me hear the ancient whisper of my ancestral
inheritance.
I've internalized whiteness so deeply,
so often,
that I am my own oppressor most times.
I am done with self-hatred,
shame,
and a push to assimilate.
I am here because of the women who came
before me with
Strength, rage and sadness in their bones.

I am only here because trauma and pain of my
ancestors.
The dawn is coming
And I am the dawn.

Vulture

I rip open the flesh from my chest,
pull the strands of meat from my hungry ribs.
The tissue tears like parchment paper.
I am my own vulture.
Through gritted teeth and
bloodied gums,
the maniacal smile spreads across my face.
The cadaverous pallor eases down my once
golden skin.
Watch me tear myself apart.
Pick
       The
           Scabs
From my healing heart.
I can never allow myself to heal or be whole.

Black Widow

Black widows spill from my pink slit,
Venomous to any who enter.
Do not stay too long.
Her teeth are sharp;
Thirsty for your blood.
Hungry for your manhood.
I
      Will
            Emasculate
                  You.

Furious Chaos

5

My furious chaos
Quakes with stimulation
Brings the flames from the soles of my feet.
Rising into the softness of my belly,
My furious chaos writhes with satisfaction.
Pounding my heartbeat in my ears.
Keeping in time with hummingbird wings.
My jaw so tense, it cracks my teeth
Furious
        Furious
                Furious
Chaos
Released.
I breathe heavily to sleep.

Waves

I'm drowning in the waves of my emotion,
Trying to delicately hold my head above water
While the tsunami threatens to pull me under.
My seventh-grade swim team skills
Are no match for the tidal waves that
Crash

       Crash

              Crash against my cardboard
skull.
My throat is full of all the
Words I've had to swallow.
My wafer skin carries but a fraction of the
muscle I need
For the grief inside the well of my heart.
I am only bones floating in water.
I am losing myself in all the things I don't say.
My belly swells as I try to swallow
The entire ocean to overcome the tsunami.
No matter how much water I fill myself with,
It is not enough to cleanse my mind.

My Sky

Today I think I'll eat a breakfast
Of a billion stars.
I try to consume the universe
As it belongs, solely to me.
I weep under a black blue sky
Manic inside.
The stars freckle my skin.
They're trying to shine,
Bursting from within.
But I am not your dream come true
Or what you wish for upon a star.
I cannot offer a fairy tale ending.
I am an indigo soul, with no desire to change.

I Am Always Dying

I am always dying
But I keep going on.
My soul is a restless hunger.
752 tsunamis I have cried,
And they did not drown me.
My persistent flame reignites.
I was not lost in the fire,
I was built from it.
I have been buried under years of ash.
I scream off key,
With a voice that sounds like it's been gargling
gasoline.
It is with tar running through my blood
That I am weighed down.
But I keep going on.
I was born with my fist in the air!
I am the claw end of a hammer,
With the abrasiveness of sandpaper.
Be careful how you fix your mouth in my
direction;
I might just knock it back in place.

Cold

Icicles threaten to harden my heart
Frost paints a veneer on its windows
I cannot see beyond the frigidity
To find the warmth in my soul
I shiver, though my blood runs hot
A malignant freeze finds a home in my spirit.
I am weary.
Turning cold, resistant and unbreakable
I refuse the comfort of warmth
Because I want to know that I can be rigid.
I want to know that the icicles can help me build
my boundaries.
When I am warm, I am weak.
I do not want to give in to the world anymore.

Silent, No More

I am loud
In a world that tries to minimalize my voice
After decades of being told to be quiet.
Silence my thoughts,
Silence my boldness,
Silence, even the guttural laughter
That dare erupt from happiness.
Don't be too loud.
Silence the part of you that dares defy
The polite rules of society.
I cannot
I will not
do this anymore.
Expect to hear me shouting when waves of
injustice preside.
Expect to hear me bellow when I try to slay my
dragons,
Before they spill out of my mouth.
My cries will rattle the windows of my house
Until the panes split and the walls shake.
I will be silent no more.

Fireflies

I do not own enough fireflies
To light my way home
In the darkest woods,
The voices speak to me.
Reminding me of each and every failing.
Anxiety grabs my throat,
Crushing it with ease.
I am nothing.
Nothing.
I do not deserve to exist.
My fireflies dimly tempt me back home.
A spark here,
a twinkle there.
Guiding me back to my safe space,
The last place I could find solace.
Not too many people are invited into my home.
Not because I have anything to hide,
but because I have everything to protect.
Anxiety is the unwelcome guest that threatens
my home
Depression is its twin flame, tagging along to
bring destruction.
They have no place in my home and I refuse to
let them in.

My fireflies know I find comfort in their
knowledge of the path;
Together we fly home.

The Struggle

It is in the silence between the chaos
That I remember who I am.
The constant questioning of validity in my
existence.
Doubt is my faithful companion.
Never knowing if I am enough
Never feeling that I am enough
I have set impossible standards for myself,
Then let the disappointment rage when I do not
meet them.
Daily, the heaviness in my heart
Threatens to drop into my stomach.
It is the stone I cannot swallow,
The ache I cannot digest.
The shame of all my failings
Lick at my spine.

My Own Music

I cannot be
The background noise in my own life
I cannot settle
With being unsettled.
I will not be the white noise
In my own heart.
To be the hum between my loves,
I must know my melody.
Make myself into music,
before the static takes over.
How can I not see that I am deserving
of being the main chorus in my own song?

Magic

Magic demands awareness
I must have faith.
You have to believe in magic
to create it into reality.
Preparation within ourselves
Allows our magic to manifest.
What are your poisonous resistances?
How do you impede yourself?
Know and acknowledge them.
Then, surrender.
Stay out of your own way
and let the magic do what it does.
The universe wants you to have your magic.
Will you get out of your own way and receive it?

Introvert

I am an introvert with anxiety.
I will talk your ear off, overshare,
Be super bubbly
And then hope I never run into you again.
I am caffeine, lipstick and chaos.
I am the highest of highs
And the lowest of lows.
I recharge in solitude.
I am black glitter and cat eye glasses.
I am a colony of bats,
Waiting for darkness to take flight.
I am a new adventure between the covers of a
book.
I am an empath; I guard my energy.
I am, still, an introvert with anxiety.

Lost Hope

My blood, though I was the innocent,
rains down from my wrists.
It feels effervescent in my soul,
Extracting my silence, and
All I can manage is a sigh…
And in the light of day
I know I'll regret this mistake.
I've broken my tiny glass heart.
And with these shards,
I fracture with pain.
The splinter of my bones
punctures my paper skin
until I hold
nothing more
and wilt.
An empty vessel of lost hope.

Imposter

Today I was asked, "Are you a writer?"
And with all the courage I could muster,
I mumbled, "I pretend I am."
As if the thousands of words
that have colored my thoughts to paper,
never appeared.
Because, no, though I write, I do not consider
myself a writer.
I pretend I am.

Bigger Aim

They've said, every day,
Your life is just going to be this way.
I reject the notion
That my life has no forward motion.
You will eat your words;
As I slice through them with skill.
The sharpest sword.
I rise from beneath your limitation.
Trust me,
I carry the highest level of intimidation.
Don't you dare say
That my life will always be this way.
My spirit fights for a bigger aim,
Higher than your miniscule mind
Could ever claim

Sunken

If I am the captain
then, this
THIS
is a sinking ship

Home

When you see my tears
Sprawl across my face
You turn away.
They remind you that I am human.
I have to invert my ribcage
To force my heart to beat,
Most days.
I point to my chest,
and remind myself,
my heart is my home.

Explosion

I leave the gas on,
breathing through the fumes.
Lightheaded halos
dancing on the ceiling
Flick a spark,
and I explode into 10.2 million pieces
752 for you.
I turn to stardust, instead of ash.
I belong to the sky.

In the Silence

My poetry isn't always pen to paper.
Sometimes it is the exhalation
Of a job well done,
Or the sweat of my brow from working hard
To provide for my family.
It's the late nights when sleep doesn't want to
come,
Because there are so many chores to be done,
Books to be read,
Floors to mop,
Dishes to wash,
And mouths to feed…
It's the oh-my-gosh-what-day-is-it.
My poetry is the grind of my life,
Trying to keep everyone afloat.
Juggle all the balls and not let a single one fall.
Eventually, they will…
Hopefully, only one at a time.
My poetry is in the ache of my feet,
the cracking of my back,
and when my brain is too tired
to form a coherent thought,
my poetry resides in the silence
between words.